ASTROLOGY

Embrace Your Sign and Play to Your Astrological Strengths

Publications International, Ltd.

Interior and cover art:

Shutterstock.com

Louis Weber, CEO
Publications International, Ltd.
8140 Lehigh Avenue
Morton Grove, IL 60053

ISBN: 978-1-64558-120-8

Manufactured in China.

8 7 6 5 4 3 2 1

Let's get social!

○ @Publications_International

❶ @PublicationsInternational

www.pilbooks.com

CONTENTS

"ASTROLOGY IS A LANGUAGE.
IF YOU UNDERSTAND THIS
LANGUAGE, THE SKY
SPEAKS TO YOU."

— DANE RUDHYAR

ACROSS THE UNIVERSE

If you simply glance at the sky, each morning and night will blend in unison; every new day seemingly like the one before.

———————————

However, if you take a long pause when you're outside and absorb all the sky offers, you will see a different scene painted with every passing moment. Whether it is glinting strokes of sunlight or stars sporadically brushed across the atmosphere, if you look closely, there is always a new painting to gaze upon.

Astrology is using the meaning found in the sky as an explanation of our attributes. It's the study of the Sun, Moon, and Stars and the belief that their movements make up our character. Its purpose is to be a map as we navigate the labyrinth of life.

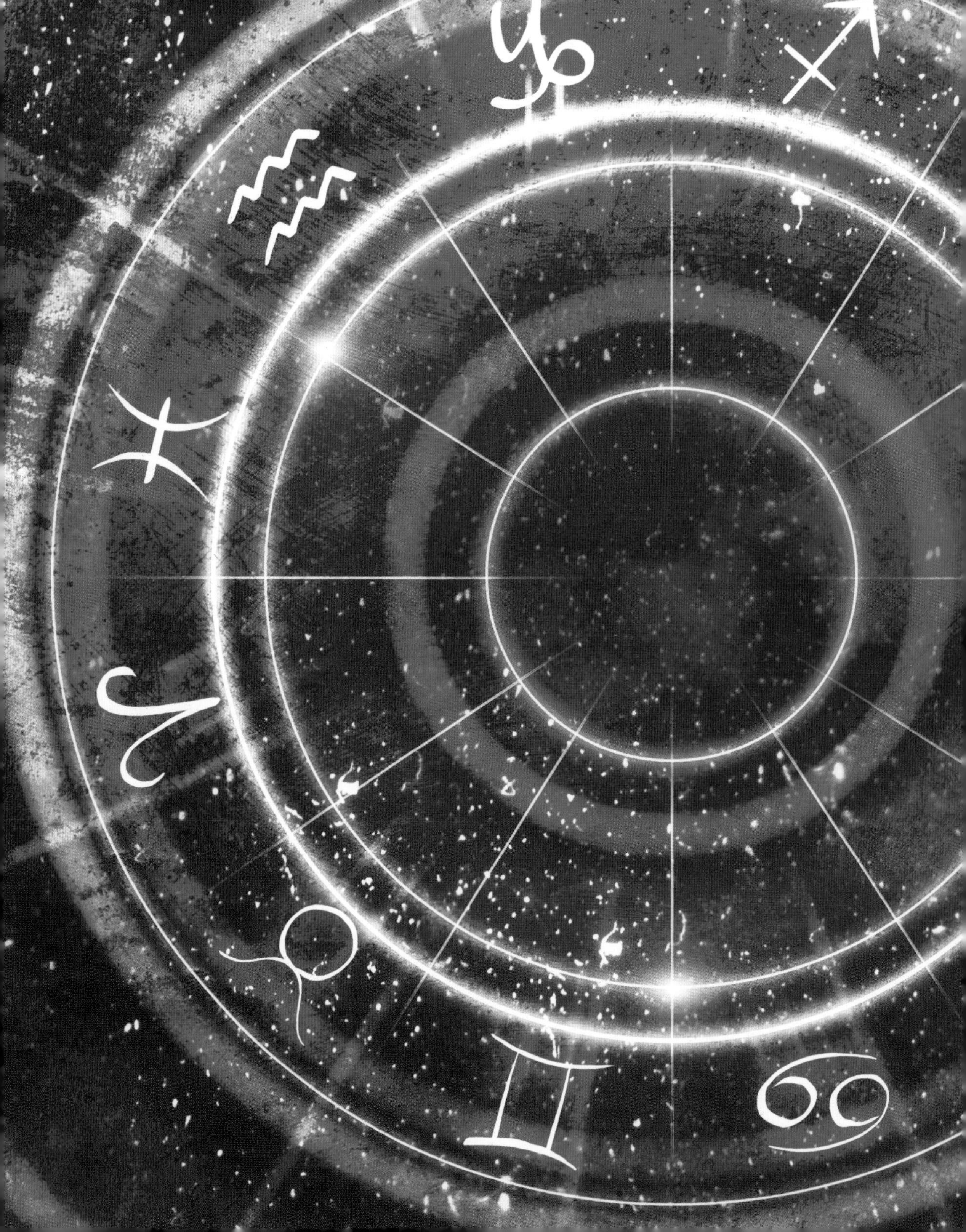

12 Zodiac Signs:

Aries ♈
Taurus ♉
Gemini ♊
Cancer ♋
Leo ♌
Virgo ♍
Libra ♎
Scorpio ♏
Sagittarius ♐
Capricorn ♑
Aquarius ♒
Pisces ♓

The alignment of the cosmos can explain our Zodiac sign and the personality traits we embody from it. However, our Zodiac sign is only the flare that escapes the surface of the Sun; it is an outlier of understanding ourselves.

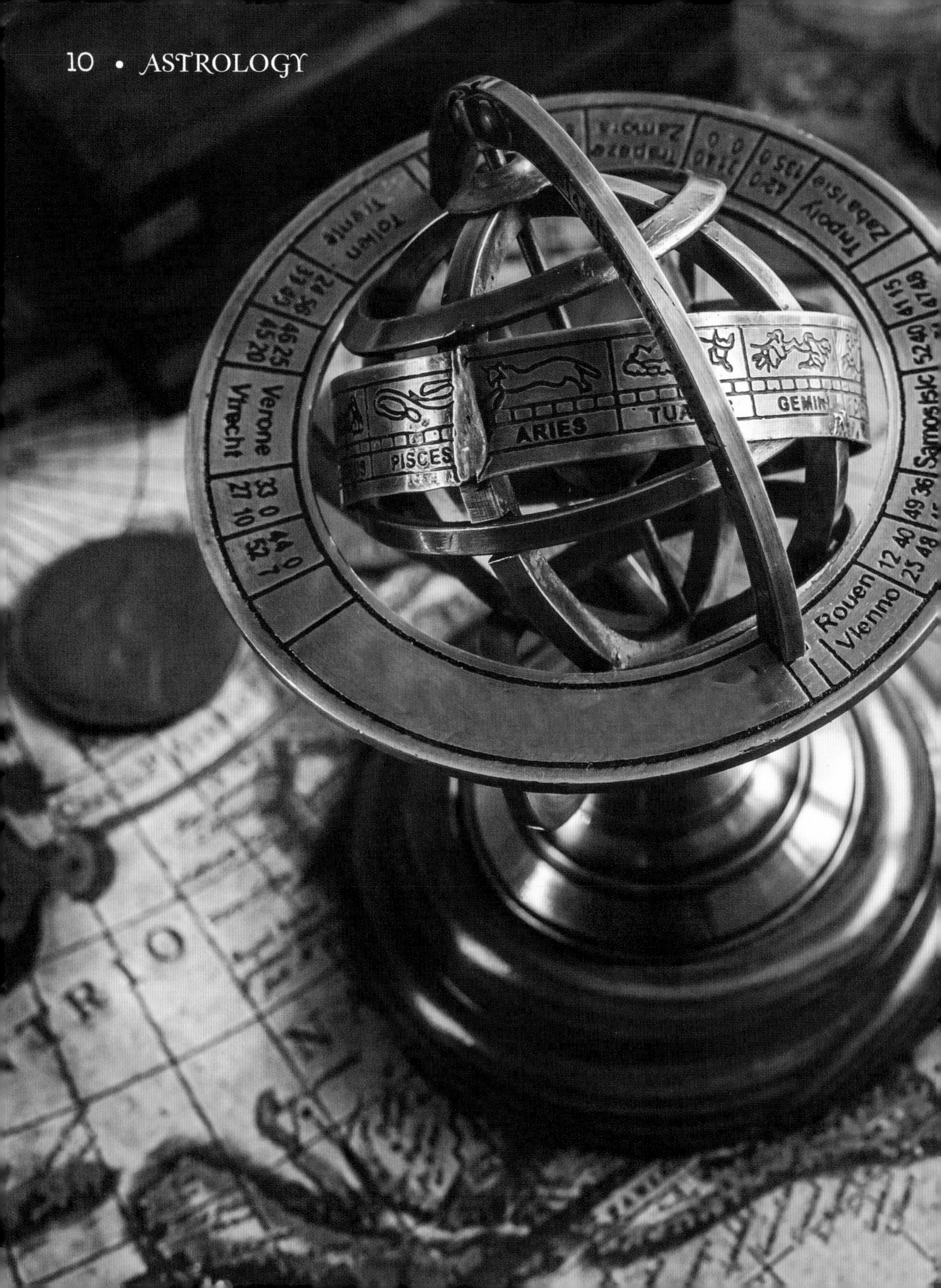
Verone
Vtrecht
PISCES
ARIES
Rouen
Vienno

The Sun, Moon, and Rising signs influence our daily lives.

Each sign is fundamental to comprehending our inner and outer layers because when the layers are assembled, our notable strengths and shortcomings come forth.

It's essential to note that astrology does not dictate who you are or can be, but rather how you react and deal when conflicts arise. This book is only a snippet of a vast subject; it is a starting tool to understand your signs. With a new perspective of yourself, this is the year to begin again.

A Cosmic Beginning

The beginning
of a new year means
a reset of our resolutions.

A conquest to read more or spend less, we try to sew up what has been unraveling. Nonetheless, many of us fail to maintain a tenacious grip on our list. It slips through our fingers, and we eventually begin to stumble over what we let go.

Looking at the cosmos is a way to understand what lies ahead.

As we move on from the teen years of the 21st century and enter the twenties, we must keep in mind the past decade and the resolutions we promised to ourselves. With lessons learned from the past, we can create a new template for the future.

Our narrative is a manifestation of life's ups and downs, but how did we get to the ups and downs? What leads to where we are? Most importantly, where can we go?

Following the path of the Sun, Moon, and Stars will lead you to the answer.

You're at the gate to your next destination, whether that is a career, relationship, or a deeper you; your Sun, Moon, and Rising signs are the plane to get you there.

"THREE THINGS CANNOT
BE LONG HIDDEN: THE
SUN, THE MOON, AND
THE TRUTH."

– BUDDHA

SUN SIGN

At the center of our universe lies the Sun; its celestial body is the essence as to why we continue breathing. With every breath, we can thank the Sun, because at its center is all of us. Each one of us has a Sun sign; it signifies the core of our character.

Every year the Sun passes through the 12 signs of the Zodiac.

When someone asks, "What's your sign?" they are likely referring to your Sun sign. Your Sun sign can be configured by determining where the position of the Sun was on the day and month you were born. It's how you know you're a Virgo rather than a Libra.

It represents the broad scope of our personality. It's like picking up a book and reading the inside cover.

We have an idea of what the genre and plot will be; if we're reserved or gregarious; if we have analytical or creative thinking. The Sun sign holds our unique characteristics and lays out the groundwork to better understand ourselves.

It's key to note the Sun sign isn't the only determining factor of our personality traits, because when we read the pages, we begin to interpret them differently.

"EVERYONE IS A MOON,
AND HAS A DARK SIDE
WHICH HE NEVER
SHOWS TO ANYBODY."

— MARK TWAIN

MOON SIGN

When the Sun dissolves into the horizon and the tide increases in the peak of darkness, we know the Moon has found its home in the sky. With our Sun sign, we can't conceal the traits others see; however, our Moon sign represents a different part of ourselves.

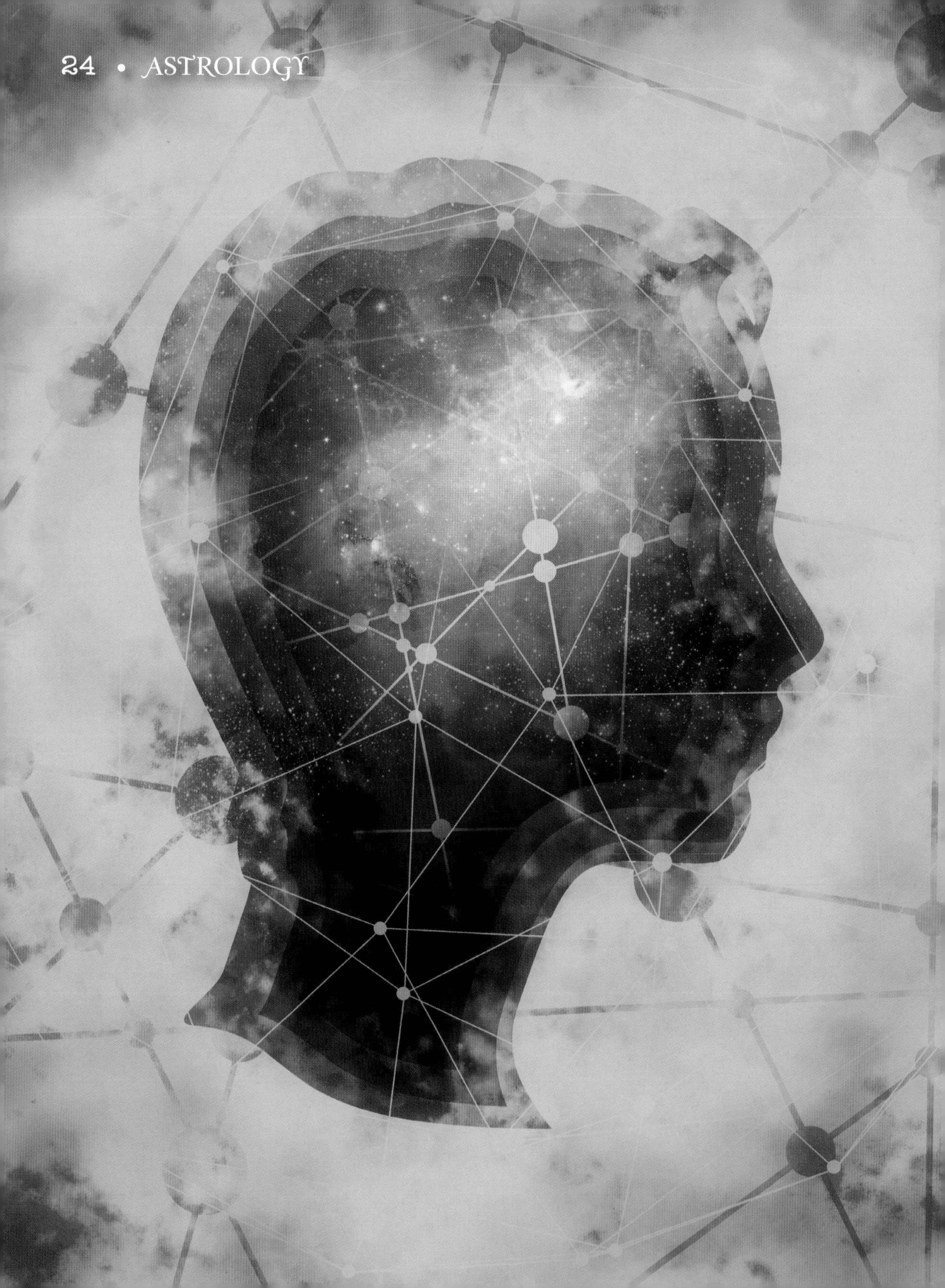

Just like the dark side of the Moon, we all have a private and hidden side. The Moon sign turns the cover to our emotional and inner pages.

Your Moon sign can explain the reason why someone notices you tend to change when they grow closer to you. If you're struggling with your identity, look up the characteristics of your Moon sign; it unlocks your inner emotions and can explain the qualities that differentiate you from your Sun sign.

The Moon sign can be determined by which of the twelve Zodiac signs the Moon traveled through on the date and time of your birth.

RISING SIGN

While the Sun sign is the inside cover, and the Moon sign is the pages within, the Rising sign is the book's cover.

When we assess a book's art and title before picking it up, we are judging how it comes across to us. The Rising sign represents our spontaneous reactions and how people perceive us from them. It is the outer shell of our dynamic layers; it's the very surface of who we are as a whole.

Your Rising sign is the sign that was rising over the eastern horizon when you were born. When determining your Rising sign, you'll need to know the exact time of your birth, because the signs of the Zodiac change every two hours.

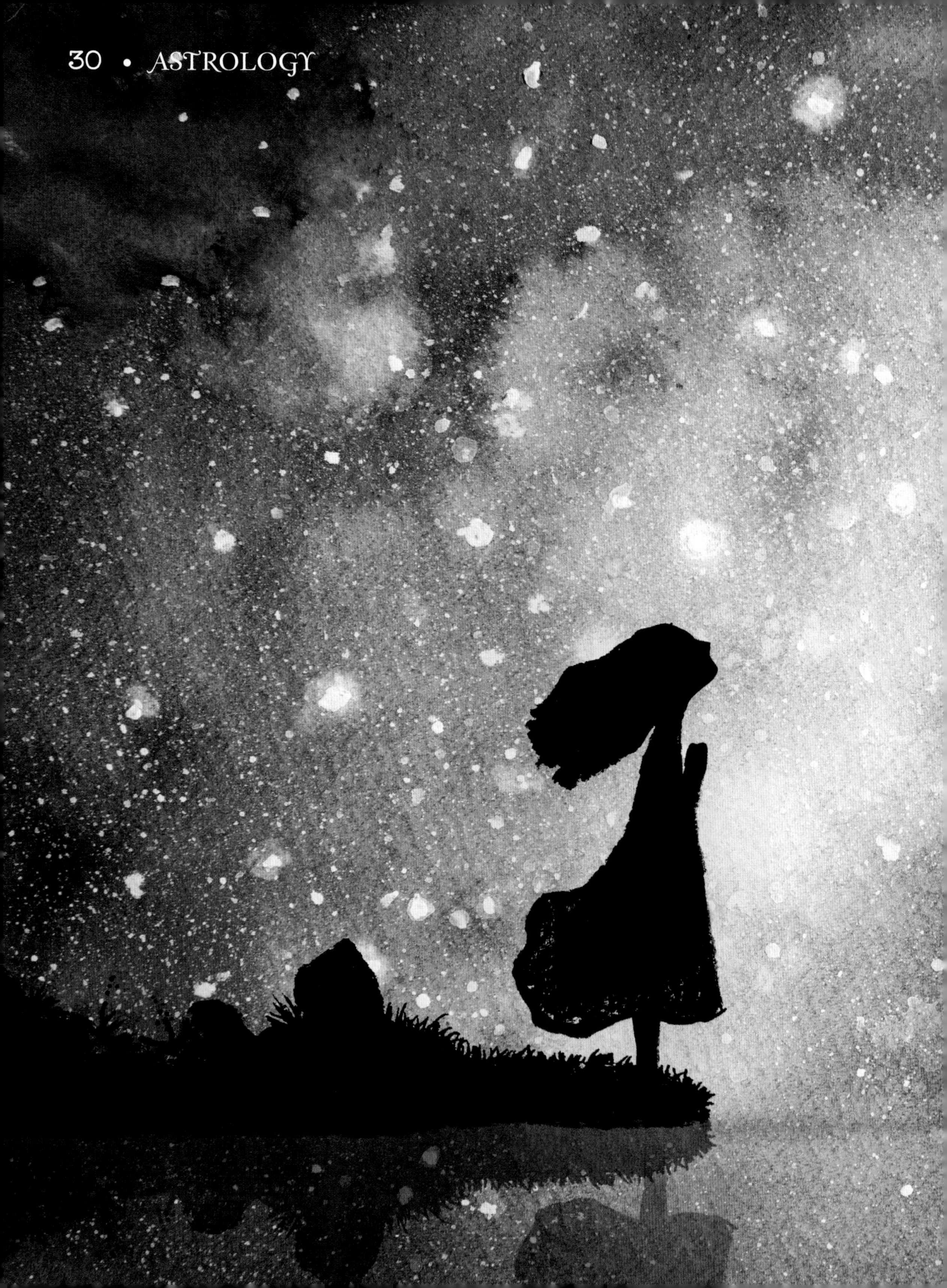

If you don't associate
with your Sun sign, then you
should look toward the other
signs as they expand upon
your characteristics. When
someone you know displays
similar personality traits to
you but are not within your
Sun sign, it's likely both of
you have the same Moon or
Rising sign.

**We all pride ourselves
in individuality because
not one of us is alike
in the world.**

Understanding how all three
signs harmonize together
will help you distinguish your
uniqueness from other people
and allow you to blossom
from it.

ZODIAC ELEMENTS

We are dependent on the Earth's primitive elements: Fire, Earth, Water, and Air. It's how we keep warm, stay grounded, drink, and breathe.

Every day we are entangled in these elements not only because they are necessary to our survival, but they carry distinct traits. Split into four groups, each element rules three signs. Signs under the same element have similar characteristics.

THE FIRE SIGNS

Aries, Leo, and Sagittarius.

Whether it's a candle lit on the kitchen table or the crackle of logs shifting, we can sense when there is fire around us. Fire signs, wherever they go, are known to light up a room with their exuberant and warm personality. When it comes to taking on projects or roles of leadership, they have a driving spark to complete it with precision.

However, these signs must only take on what they can handle. While a little spark can be harmless, a fire that grows out of control is destructive.

THE EARTH SIGNS

Taurus, Virgo, and Capricorn.

Gravity is why everyone stands upright. Like the magnetic force, Earth signs keep themselves grounded. They are loyal and don't float away from people who have stuck by their side. They are known to be practical, because they always assess the most logical track before they begin their journey.

While it is canny to know the map before setting afoot, Earth signs can become too focused on the route and forget why they began the journey.

THE WATER SIGNS

Pisces, Cancer, and Scorpio.

The clarity of an ocean or pool is why people can't avoid anything underneath them. Just like the transparency of water, Water signs can easily sense when someone has gone under the current; they are emotionally intuitive and empathetic to how other people are feeling. Like the constant flow of the water, they are ambitious and run toward their dreams.

However, sometimes water can become trapped in a puddle. For Water signs to avoid a creative rut, they must find other sources nearby to keep them fluid.

"My wife's an Earth sign. I'm a Water sign. Together we make mud."

— Henry Youngman

THE AIR SIGNS

Aquarius, Libra, and Gemini

Depending on where you are, the air movement will fluctuate; it can be a warm spring breeze or a powerful gust of wind. Air signs are known to be charming; they can captivate you with just a few words, and other times they will take your breath away.

Despite how pleasant a night breeze may seem, Air signs have a tendency to be deceptive. Sometimes the wind is so faint people don't realize it swooped past them.

"I WILL LOOK ON THE
STARS AND LOOK ON THEE,
AND READ THE PAGE OF
THY DESTINY."

— LETITIA ELIZABETH
LANDON

STARGAZING

Throughout the night, stars gently inch their way across the atmosphere. Their movement so slow, it's almost untraceable. However, they're always there, and no matter where we are by nightfall, we can find them illuminating the sky.

Stars are more than a concoction of expanding dust and gas; every star is part of a collection of stars that make up something larger. It's when we are lost at sea, that we use the stars to find our way home.

Our Zodiac signs are written in the stars.

The galaxy is made up of intertwining lights that create our constellations. The Zodiac signs are based on twelve constellations, which the Sun and Moon travel through every year.

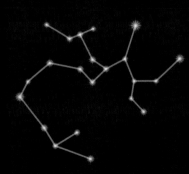

Aries

Leo

Sagittarius

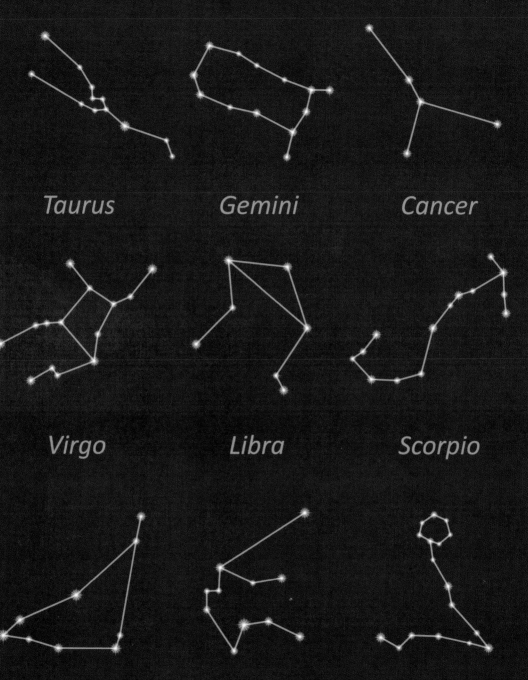

Taurus   Gemini   Cancer

Virgo   Libra   Scorpio

Capricorn   Aquarius   Pisces

ARIES
(March 21 - April 19)

Symbol: The Ram
Ruling planet: Mars
Element: Fire

Aries, the first sign of the Zodiac, coincides with the emergence of spring. Every year, their intertwinement triggers the sprouting of buds and new beginnings.

Aries

Like someone who begins a voyage, you are eager to see what awaits ahead; nothing will interfere when you're hurtling toward your goals. You embody the traits of the Ram; your exuberant personality encourages you to continue running, even if it is to the unknown.

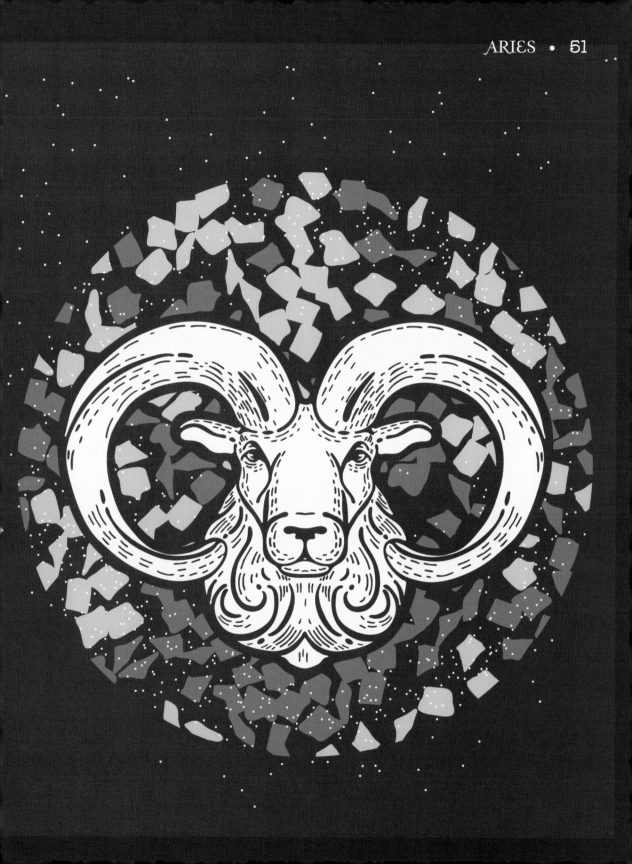

Aries is ruled by Mars, the planet of raging fire and bolstering energy.

The rising heat of Mars can explain your drive for spontaneous adventures. When the risks you take work in your favor, you feel empowered.

Not only are you the first in the Zodiac chart, but you strive to be first. Your confidence is why you are willing to be the one to drive past a roadblock sign when most people would turn around. Your willingness to bet on yourself will guide you to alternative paths along the way.

You're a spotlight stealer.

You are an advocate leader and people listen to what you have to say. As someone who usually volunteers to be the pilot on new projects, you would rather go at it alone as others have a tendency to mess it up.

When rushing through projects at full speed, you can become impatient with others. As a leader, it can be difficult to concede to another position, but make sure you allow other people to be involved in your decision process. It's important to have independence but be careful with always putting yourself first or others will leave you behind.

Life is always exhilarating with an Arian.

When it comes to your relationships, don't sacrifice your individuality for the sake of pleasing someone else. People will come and go; it's through your courage, that you find the ability to step away from those who hold you back.

This year is about balancing out your priorities. Continue trying new things and keep in mind to follow through when you take something on.

TAURUS
(April 20 – May 20)

Symbol: The Bull
Ruling planet: Venus
Element: Earth

As a Taurus, unlike the unpredictable Aries, you like order and are most relaxed from the comfort of your home.

Taurus

You resemble the qualities of your symbol the Bull. A Bull with its herd is kind and gentle. However, when it becomes angry, steam begins to build and its nostrils flare. As lessons learned from inside the ring, it's best no one goes up against you during a fight.

Venus, the planet of love and beauty, rules over Taurus.

You enjoy the finer things in life, such as elegant decorations, delicious food, and traveling to a new city. You have a sensitive side that you share with only people you let in.

You plan out your steps before acting; impulsiveness isn't like you. You're persistent when it comes to going after what you want, and nothing will sidetrack you on your way to glory.

Your decisions are not based on impractical solutions; there is logical evidence that backs them up.

You are known to be dependable as others lean on you for advice.

You can be stubborn though. It can be challenging for people to get you outside your comfort zone. You know what you like, and there are few people who can steer you far from that direction.

When it comes to relationships, you're romantic and passionate toward your partner. Rather than showcasing it to the world, you show it in private. You would rather stay at home watching a movie with someone than go out partying.

Looking toward the rest of the year, don't get stuck in a rut. Sometimes you avoid change when you become too comfortable, but change is not necessarily a bad thing. You can benefit from new lifestyles you grow into.

GEMINI
(May 21 - June 20)

Symbol: The Twins
Ruling planet: Mercury
Element: Air

A Gemini's energy
surges with quick-witted
words and intellectually
curious thoughts.

Gemini

Geminis are known to be versatile like their symbol the Twins. Your duality allows you to take on a plethora of activities. You'll always have something to discuss, whether it's the recipe you're learning, the team you're rooting for, or the new book you purchased.

Mercury, the planet
of communication,
explains your
conversational nature.

You can talk for hours on a
variety of subjects, which is
why people will gravitate toward
you; they're never bored when
you're near.

Your gregarious
personality lights
up a room that has been
kept in the dark. Your
kind and charming
attributes tends to warm
people up when they had
been chilly further away.

You are smart and cheerful. However, you are fickle. While most of the time you are a magnetic presence, you can also drive people away who don't get your wit with sarcastic comments.

As someone who loves to talk, you also love to gossip.

Your inclination of loving drama from a tabloid, can lead you to be two-faced. While you may not mean to leak secrets, you will bring up any information when a conversation goes south.

You can ignite a spark between yourself and any person who comes along. The thing with sparks is they either go up in a blaze or die quickly. Your problem isn't obtaining a relationship, it's staying in it.

As a Gemini, your vivacious persona will lead you to accomplish your ultimate agenda.

You cling to change because you are willing to open yourself to new possibilities. Just don't steer yourself too far off the map in the upcoming year.

CANCER

(June 21 – July 22)

Symbol: The Crab
Ruling planet: The Moon
Element: Water

Cancerians are
caretakers. They enthrall
every person they meet
through their welcoming and
compassionate personality.

Cancer

Like Crabs, you are fluid between the sea and the shore. As much as you love being on the surface with everyone, you are known to hide in the depths of the water when someone sets you off.

The ruling Moon can explain why you're overwhelmed with emotions

When the Moon finally becomes transparent, so do you; a sensitive side is intrinsic to Cancer. It's why you may make decisions with intuition rather than logic.

You are known as the nurturer of your friend group. When the time has surpassed all of you, you are the one initiating plans for everyone to come together. Hosting parties at your place is the marriage between wanting to stay home and seeing those you care about.

Your loyalty is why you never stray far from what is close to your heart; you have constant communication with your family. Even if you have come to live elsewhere, you will find yourself calling them with updates. The secure space from inside your shell makes you a homebody.

Cancer's downfall is sensitivity. You are known to misconstrue the meaning of harmless words. Don't let everything sink you, because an isolated Crab drifting alone at sea can wallow in self-pity for days before coming back to shore.

You have a protective shell, and it can be hard for someone to crack through. Once there is a fissure, your vulnerability seeps toward the sand for a person to grab. When they do make the way into your life, you will not want to let go.

People will always say things to get you down.

It's your choice to sulk or push it aside.

While dispensing largesse is something to be valued, be generous to yourself. As you set your agenda, make this year about you.

LEO
(July 23 - August 22)

Symbol: The Lion
Ruling planet: The Sun
Element: Fire

A Leo is known
to command a room
as soon as they step
inside; Leo have a
fiery and outgoing
personality.

Leo

As a Leo, you never go unnoticed. Like your symbol the Lion, everyone seems to revere you when you're close by. A Lion is the leader of the animal kingdom, and like them, royalty is just a part of who you are.

As a Leo, you are continuously glimmering, and people can't hide from your glare.

The Sun is a vital part of the solar system and your ruling planet. The planets will travel around it until the end of time; simultaneously, things will continue to revolve around you.

You are known to prove yourself. You're not afraid to go down in a burning blaze as long as you tried. With being able to risk it all, comes your courage. Not everyone can sacrifice everything, not knowing what they will get in return.

Your energy radiates the stage because you were born to be an entertainer.

It's not that you mean to be center, but eyes have already been on you. Without trying, you upstage those around you in any performance.

With royalty comes pride, and too much pride can lead to an arrogant nature. It's essential to be able to admit when you're wrong because everyone needs a little humility to keep themselves grounded.

You are passionate and exciting, and people are dazzled when they are around you.

Sunlight drips from the ceiling when someone is with you. You'll never forego passion for dullness. Life with you is far from banal.

Take this year with the same self-assurance you started with. Lions let nothing stop them, and that's what makes them a powerful animal. If you live life with confidence, this year will be yours.

VIRGO
(August 23 – September 22)

Symbol: The Virgin
Ruling planet: Mercury
Element: Earth

Virgo kicks off the end of the summer and the transformation into fall. The leaves' slow pigment change can explain a Virgo's subtle nature.

Virgo

Your symbol the Virgin represents your modesty. You are known to abide by the rules. While a moralistic attitude isn't trivial and plays a significant role in molding you, avoid living life in black and white.

The messenger planet rules over you.

Mercury can explain your wisdom and the drive you have as a perfectionist. As a doer, you are striving to get things done with precision.

Your intellectual acuity
is notable by those around
you. Your decisions are based
on analytical inferences,
because practicality is key
to you. Your choices are a
testament to how hard you
work to achieve success.

As much as you value solitude, friendship is principal. As a Virgo, you always want to help those around you, and that's what makes you dependable. Dedication is essential to your craft, and it's why you're able to persevere when others would give up.

However, your perceptiveness can make you overly critical of those around you. Overthinking situations can make you give up on something that could've been remarkable.

You are known to self-sabotage your relationships. You don't want to be hurt, so you convince yourself not to become emotionally attached; however, your mentality of not wanting to become upset, will leave you upset.

Looking toward the year,
let yourself outside of the
perimeter you set up. If you
put up a wall that comes
tumbling down, no one
wins when they are left in
crumbling pieces. Ease
yourself by removing one
brick at a time.

LIBRA
(September 23 - October 22)

Symbol: The Scales
Ruling planet: Venus
Element: Air

Libras are a convivial and harmonious bunch. Their charming presence is why they are good at keeping the peace; they don't want to be on anyone's bad side.

Libra

The Scales are your symbol, because you favor balance. To avoid conflict, you are usually the referee and want to settle whatever problem arises. You are always playing devil's advocate, because you give everyone the benefit of the doubt.

The planet of love and beauty rules over you.

Venus can explain your luxurious taste; whether it's decorating your home or putting together an outfit for work, nothing in your life will look out of place.

As a Libra, your spirit is infectious. You can make people laugh and just let loose because having fun is intrinsic to your personality. As a people pleaser, you need to keep everyone happy.

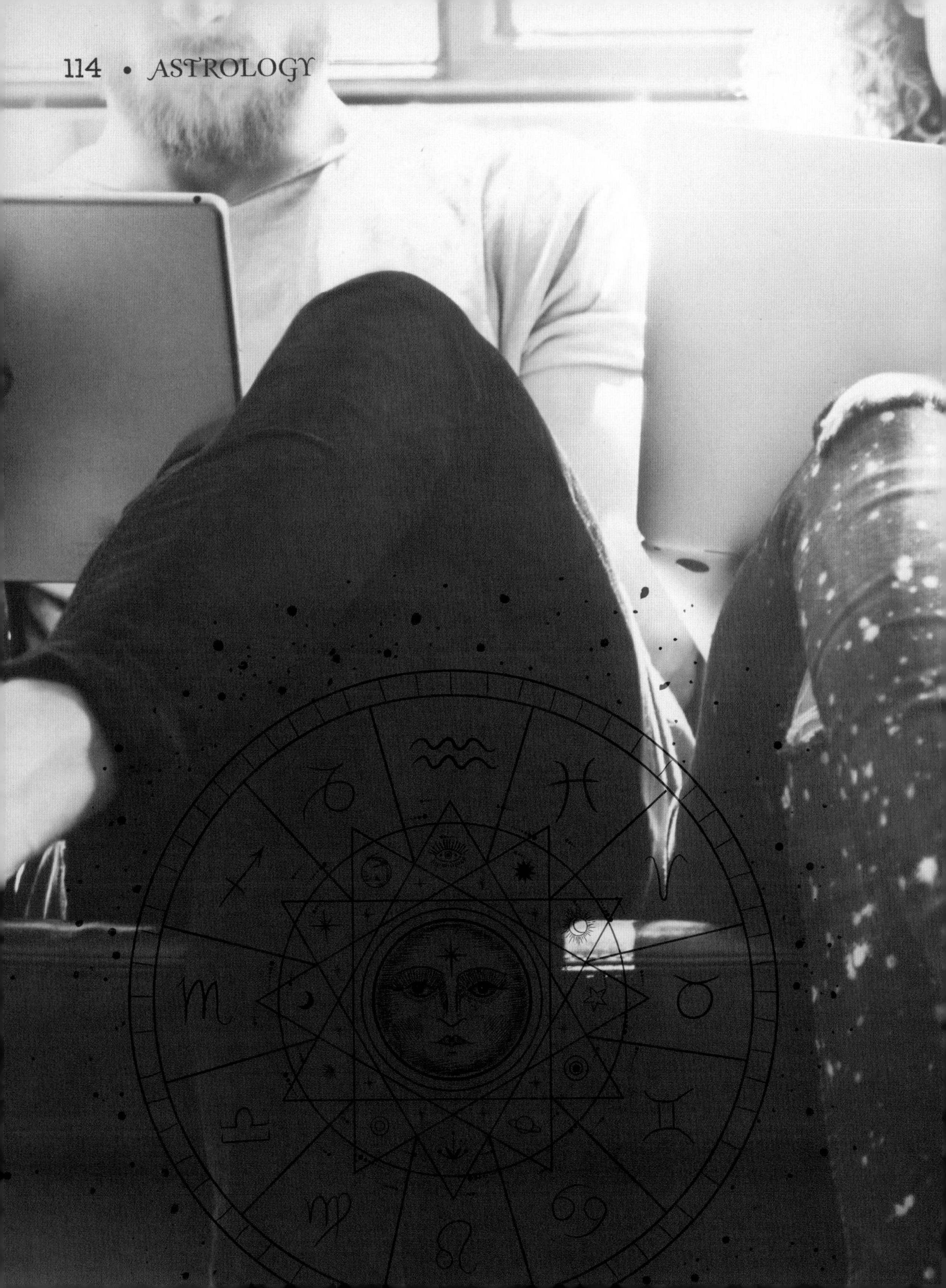

You're diplomatic and are known to settle conflicts with compromise. Your easygoing nature concurs with indecisiveness. You never want to be the determining factor when you and your friends are choosing the next adventure.

However, an easygoing personality can make you a target for a pushover. By letting people take whatever they want, you may start to hold grudges against them. Confrontation is not always a bad thing; it will allow you to settle problems a different way.

You are a romantic in relationships. You love the honey-
moon phase, and you fall fast
if you connect with a person.
However, falling fast can take
a sharp turn because once
that period starts to fade, you
move on.

This is your year of assertion. You will never get anything in life if you remain passive, and even though it's hard for you, live life by doing and not settling.

SCORPIO
(October 23 – November 21)

Symbol: The Scorpion
Ruling planet: Pluto
Element: Water

Scorpios captivate anyone who decides to intertwine their lives with them. They are instinctively passionate, which is why people are consumed with everything they have to offer.

Scorpio

A Scorpion is calm
and collected, and
like your symbol you
observe and evaluate
situations before you
strike. You are
always on high-alert
and everyone near
you is aware of your
powerful sting.

Pluto rules over you. It's known for its transformation through life and death. You are an enigma, because of your unpredictability to those around. Pluto can explain the swift change in your personality from the cycles of life.

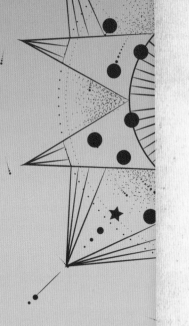

As a Scorpio, you are perceptive. You notice the tiny details in everyone and everything. With noticing the micro picture, you rationalize before making decisions. In an ideal world, everyone listens to you as you should have control over the situation.

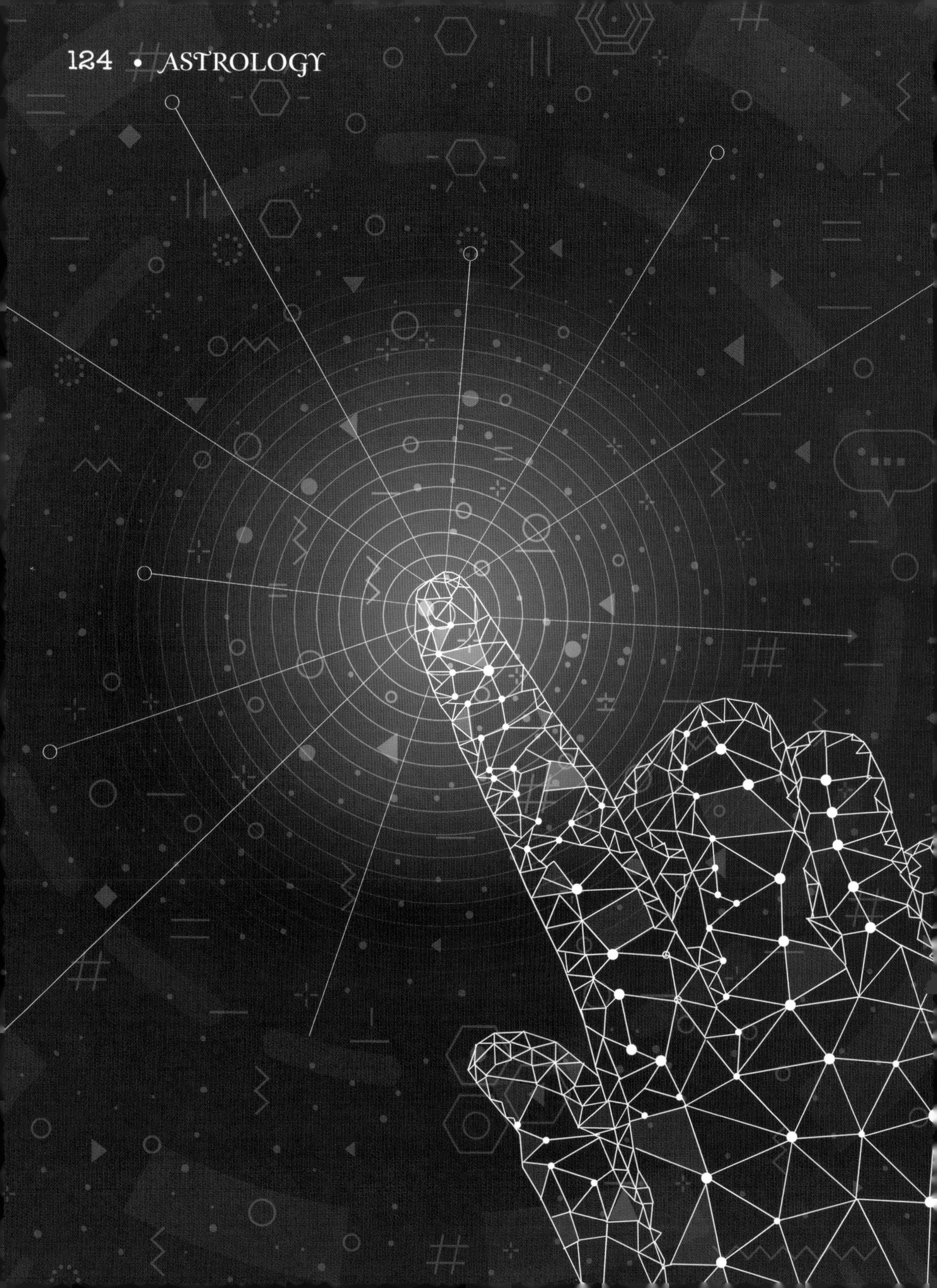

Through your intuition, you are able to understand people, and you use it to your advantage. As a resourceful person, people come to you for job advice as that is where you thrive.

The vast range of your emotions can be seen as being somewhat turbulent to others. Your devotion can be borderline possessive, and you can become suspicious of someone's actions if their motives don't seem genuine.

You are the one in charge in relationships. You won't concede that you're wrong to your partner. However, even in control, you crave passion. Intimacy is your guide to a lasting relationship.

It takes a lot for you to become vulnerable. It's important that in the year to come, you aren't in your head about everything you take on. Control can limit your opportunities to try new things, so it's essential to be able to relinquish your grip.

SAGITTARIUS
(November 22 - December 21)

Symbol: The Archer
Ruling planet: Jupiter
Element: Fire

Saggittarius coexists with the brisk temperatures that signal winter. They have a natural storytelling ability and an ebullient presence felt rooms away.

Sagittarius

When your bow is near, you aim high. A Sagittarius's symbol is the Archer, which represents your drive for adventure. As an adventure addict, outdoors is something you crave as you're usually browsing for new activities to take on.

The ruling Jupiter fuels your positive energy.

Optimism comes easy for you because with every night comes a new dawn, and you don't see it any other way. As someone who searches for the sun in the midst of a downpour, you attract lasting friendships.

When setting foot
on a new frontier,
you are eager to learn
what exists. You love to
explore different cultures
and lifestyles, which is
why you would move
to another place in
a heartbeat.

Independence is potent
for a Sagittarius. You thrive
on new possibilities, and
no one will keep you at a
standstill. You are a comical
relief to most and usually
keep everyone laughing.

You're blunt, and people
appreciate that they can
ask you something and
attain an honest answer
in return. However, your
candor can be interpreted
as impetuous, and some
people can find your
words offensive.

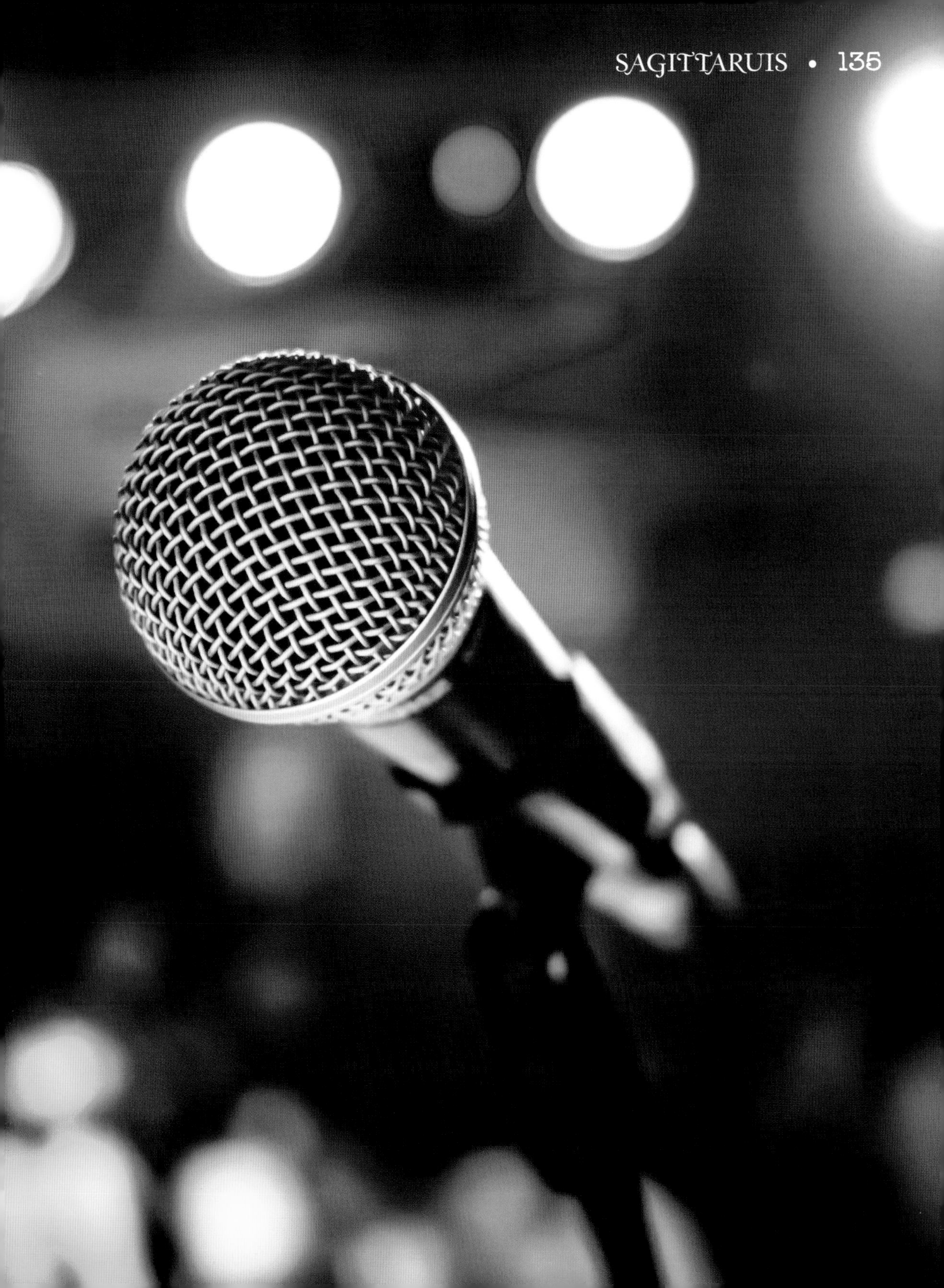

While honesty is helpful, your frankness can lead to arguments. You do flourish in monogamous relationships, but you like to have fun and have no problem flirting with people who come your way.

Use your strengths to your advantage this year. Humor goes a long way when nothing seems to be going right in the world; don't forgo your exuberance, because we all need a little fire in our lives.

CAPRICORN
(December 22 – January 19)

Symbol: The Goat
Ruling planet: Saturn
Element: Earth

When Capricorns begin an arduous journey, they are willing to endure a steady climb as long as they conquer what they come for in the end.

Capricorn

With unwavering focus, a Goat is known to stay on the same track for miles as it ascends to the top of a mountain. Like your symbol, you don't walk on man-made gravel paths, because success stems from self-discovery.

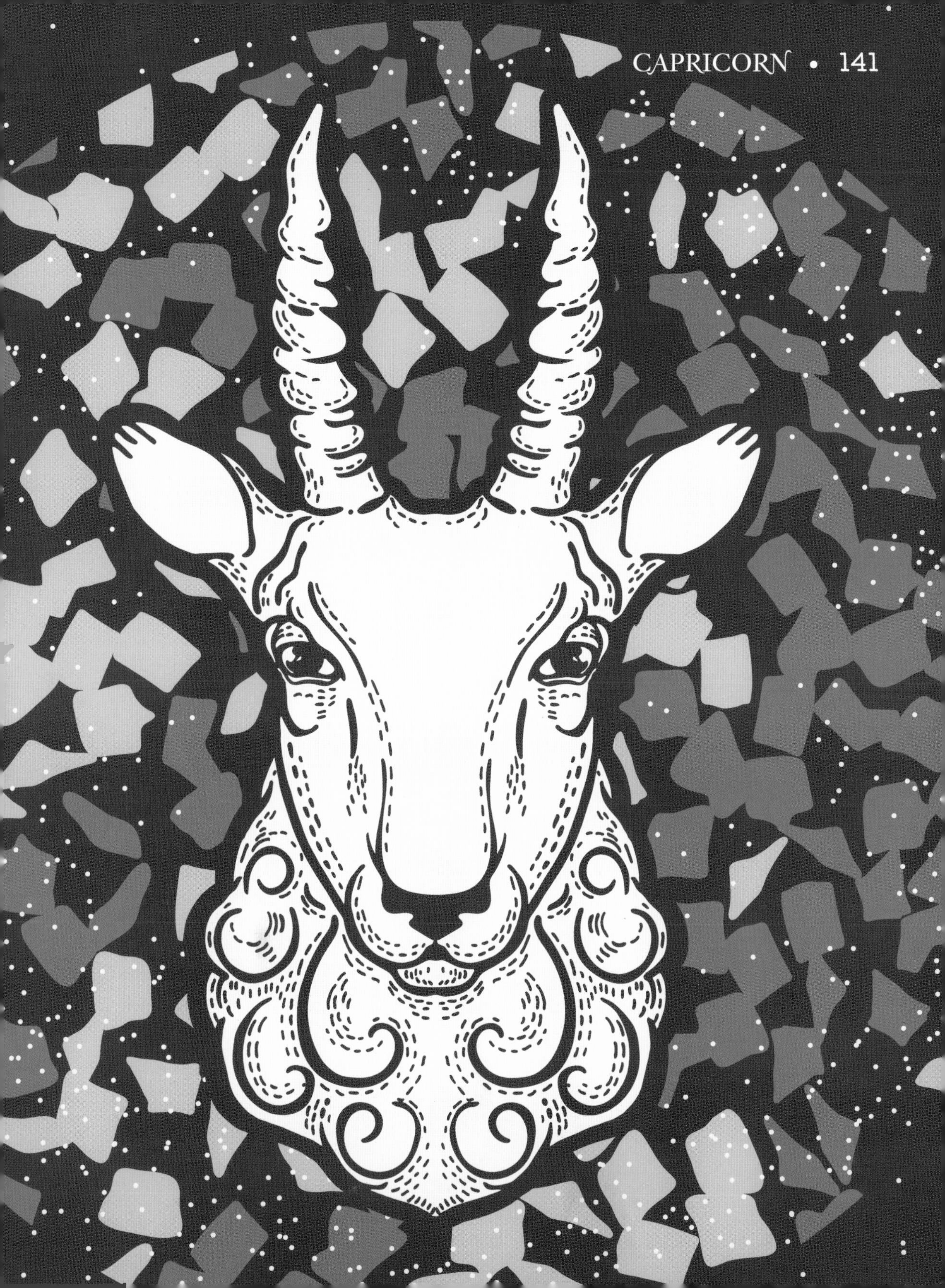

The ruling planet Saturn influences your need to discipline.

You have paternal instincts from Saturn, and your mature nature pushes you to handle chaotic situations that are in your orbit.

Undaunted, you are on a course destined for leadership. You are strong-willed and intelligent. You are one to have a firm plan and stick to it; there is little desire for a spontaneous quest when you have a map in front of you.

Success comes from persistence, one of your notable traits. You go after what you want and know cheating your way to the top is a setup for failure. Your ambitiousness sets you up for a position that people respect.

You're stubborn, and you find it's easier to get things done in solitary, which is why you reject help when it might be needed. You are known to always do things your way, which some interpret as elitism.

You want to find someone who you can be dependent on and shares similar qualities to. You are devoted to a person who is there for you; in return, nothing will deter you from leaving their side.

Remember that it is okay to let loose once in a while this year. There is no doubt that it's almost impossible to steer you off a path, but know there is an immense amount of joy to be found during a journey if you take notice.

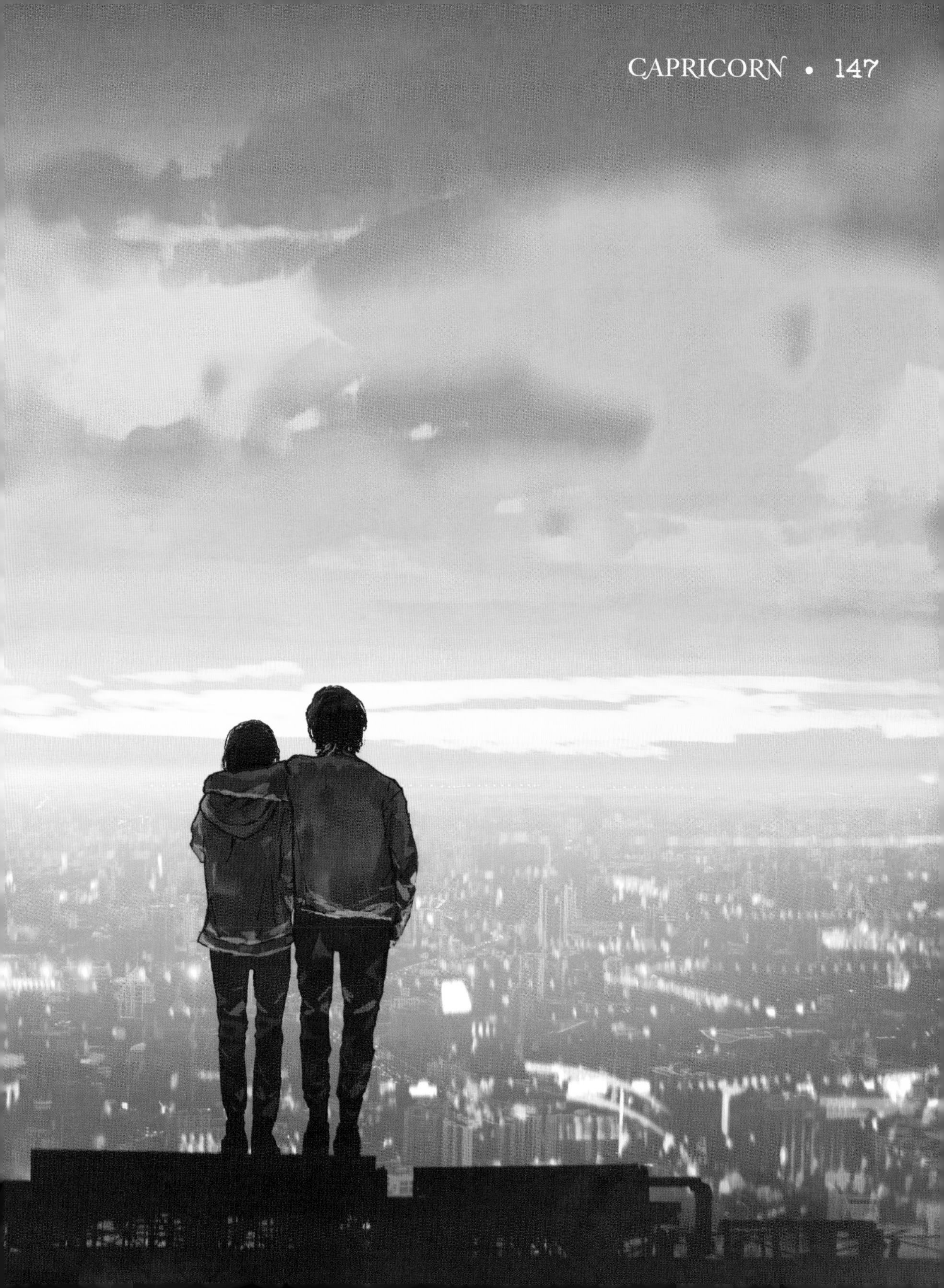

AQUARIUS
(January 20 - February 18)

Symbol: The Water Bearer
Ruling planet: Uranus
Element: Air

The unconventional
Aquarius is known as
an avant-garde individual.
Aquarians are idealists
and nothing they say
goes unnoticed.

Aquarius

You symbol, the Water Bearer, is representative of your philanthropic side. Like the Water Bearer who hands out water, you give out your truth to the world, standing up for your beliefs and criticizing those who are doing a disservice.

The planet Uranus rules over you.

Uranus is said to govern innovation and discovery. You rely on individuality to make change in the world, because those who stand out are the ones to lead it.

You are known to be
uncompromising when
it comes to your beliefs.
You are a big thinker,
and there is nothing
that is out of reach.
You feel you were put
on this world to make
an impact.

You are a free spirit,
and your uniqueness
is a magnetic force. You
are sociable; obscure
conversation topics roll
off your tongue, because you
enjoy unusual discussions.

As someone who gets
along with almost anyone,
you do tend to butt heads
with people who are narrow
minded. With having such
open opinions, you can
become pompous if people
don't view them in the
same light.

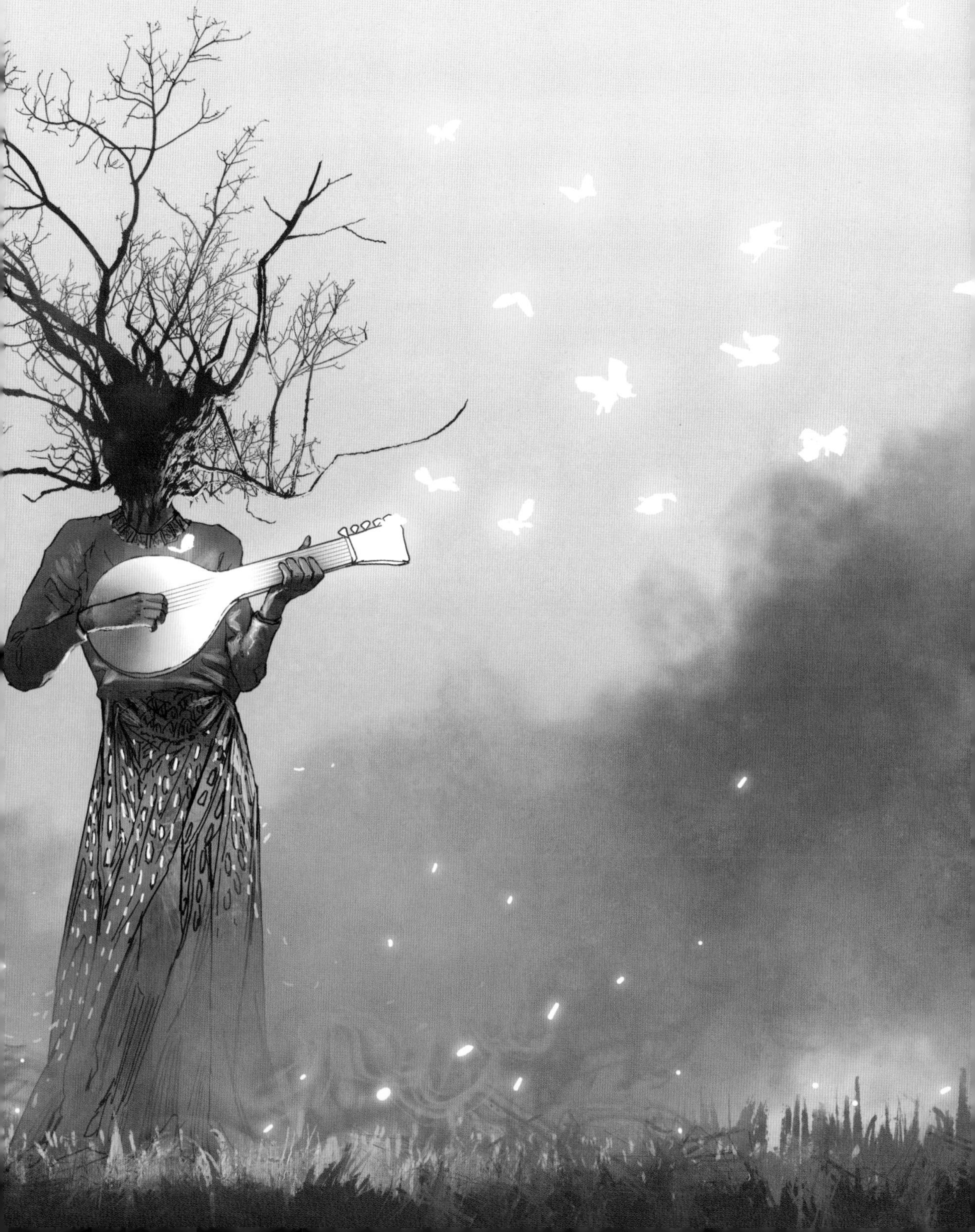

You are attracted to someone
who also cares deeply about
the world. You are laid-back
and value independence, so
lookfor someone who shares
similar qualities.

You will be able to provide calm
in the midst of chaos. this year.
Continue to spread your wisdom
and generosity; people will find
comfort when you're near.

PISCES
(February 19 – March 20)

Symbol: The Fish
Ruling planet: Neptune
Element: Water

The last sign of the Zodiac, Pisces signals the end of the circle and eventual rebirth of new beginnings.

Pisces

Fish are able to see below the surface, and like them you have impeccable intuition to how others are feeling. Fish have gills in order to adapt to their surroundings, and although you don't have gills, you are easily able to adjust when something happens.

Neptune, the planet of mystery, is your ruling planet. When you are late to gatherings or display a flaky attitude toward plans, you can put some of the blame on Neptune. The planet explains your elusive personality trait.

One of your most notable strengths is compassion. You are spiritual in a way where you can see through people. You are empathetic toward others and affection goes a long way when someone is in need of guidance.

You feel with your heart, and you have a prominent sensitive side. It explains your kindness as well as your generosity to others. You are curious and put forth all your effort when you're fully invested in something.

However, as fish tend to swim away when they are frightened, you are known to retreat. Your creative side can get the best of you, as you can be unrealistic at times when you're not in touch with reality.

When you meet someone, you fall fast and are in deep. Look out for yourself, because many times your judgement can be misplaced and you become attracted to the people who end up hurting you.

This year, use your charming presence to form new friends and relationships. As giving as you are, look out for yourself; don't let anyone take advantage of your devotion to them.

There are only two ways
to live your life:
as though nothing is a
miracle, or as though
everything is a miracle

— Albert Einstein

A Future Glance

Destiny is a vague term.

Our memoir is not handed to us at birth; there is no hidden power that has pretermined our lives. The Sun, Moon, and Stars do not make our choices; they are only a subtle way to indicate why we made them.

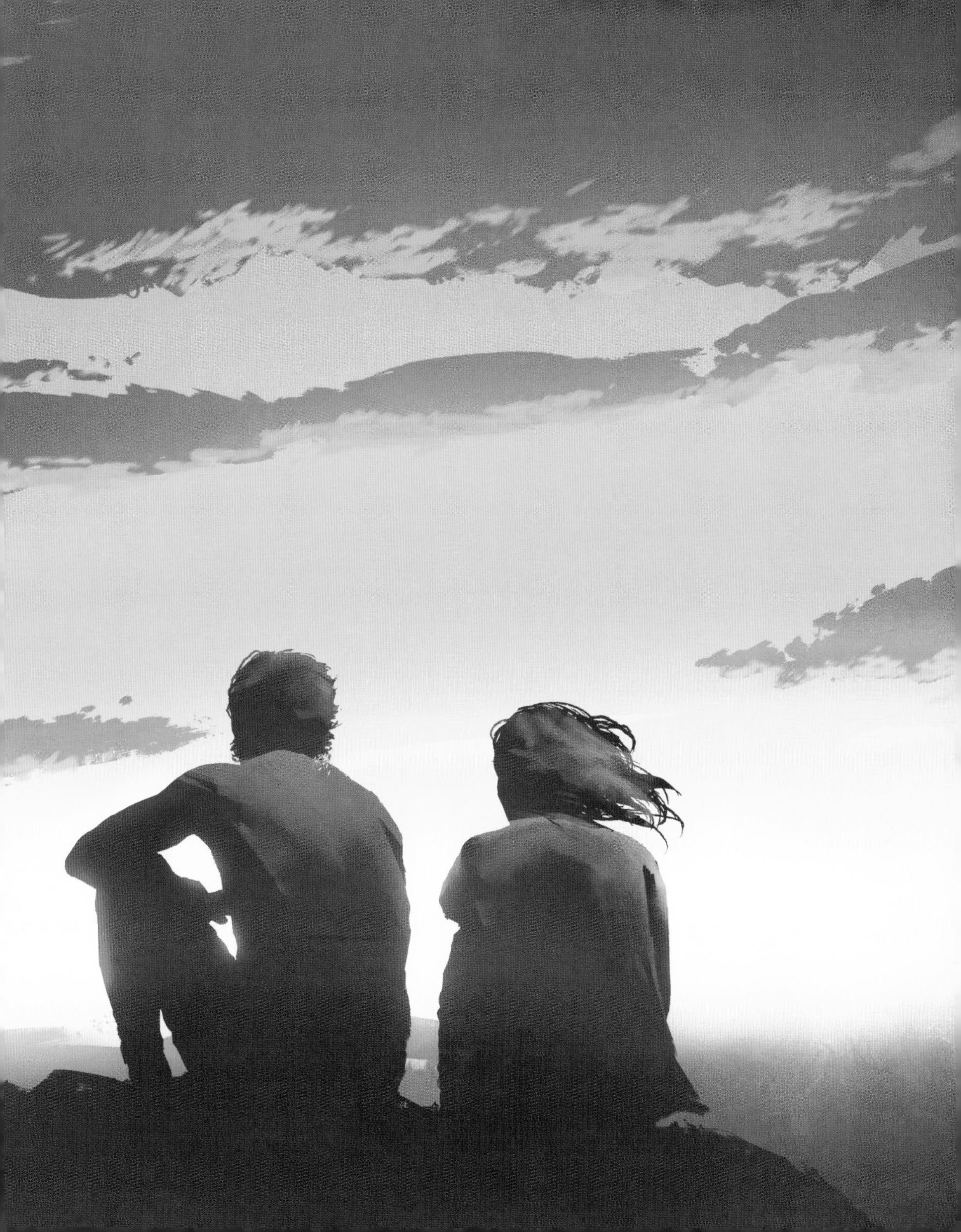

FINDING A CAREER

When we are young, the possibilities seem infinite. Our love for dance or space morph into a craving to become a ballerina or astronaut. However, few decide to pursue that path and it becomes unrealisitic later on; eventually we choose practicality.

When it comes to our career, we should be eager to get up each day; maybe not every morning but often enough. It could mean we may have to figure out what we dislike to know what we are passionate about. The most destructive thing we can do to ourselves is to stay in a career that makes us dejected.

It's okay to change courses late in life. We often endure traffic because we are accustomed to our perpetual routine. In order to find a clear road, we need to use alternative routes. If we are ready for a new career, it's up to us to make the stride.

FINDING LOVE

In the year ahead, love may be on
the radar or it may not. We value
relationships and often believe
we need them to be validated. Our
worth isn't dependent on outside
influences; don't let it define how to
live out the year.

At a specific point in life we ask
ourselves, how do we know if we
are in love? For some it might be
an instantaneous connection;
for others, it could be a steady
friendship that transitions into
something more. It's doubt
intertwined with certainty,
momentary intertwined
with permanence.

The lines can become easily blurred between bliss and tribulation when we have been in a long., bumpy relationship. When going through a breakup, know it's almost impossible to unlove someone. Love fades, but it never fully diminishes. It's how we uplift ourselves after that will allow us to move on.

Depending on your sign, you may prefer dependence and the security of having someone close, or you may prefer freedom and the enjoyment of flirtation will keep you from being tied down. Everyone is different, so listen to yourself as to what works for you.

FINDING YOURSELF

Take risks this year—especially the wrong ones; you'll be glad that you knew what was instead of wondering what could have been.

We go through periods of figuring out who we are. We try to decide what invigorates our dreams; do we pursue them or are they too far-fetched? We can be told no over and over again, and soon we will believe we are incapable.

To find yourself is to know your worth. Every time someone says no is a reason to keep striving. For us to be confident in our actions, we need to feel confident.

It comes down to when the Sun falls into oblivion against the ocean line and the stars are uncovered, we can see all of our potential. The myriad lights of the night constitute all that we can be.

"THE UNIVERSE IS NOT OUTSIDE OF YOU. LOOK INSIDE YOURSELF; EVERYTHING THAT YOU WANT, YOU ALREADY ARE."

— RUMI

A New You

Every year, we begin to deconstruct ourselves and confront the miniscule issues that we have shelved away. If you want to change an aspect in your life, don't wait for dust to settle before getting to it.

We are constantly evolving. Evolving into relationships and out of them; starting new careers or returning to old ones; meeting new people and leaving others behind. Embrace evolution because without growth we are static.

Astrology is the beginning of understanding our choices. We each have quirks we like and would prefer to change. We should embrace every part of our sign. Our strengths and shortcomings make up who we are, and we need both to ensure balance.

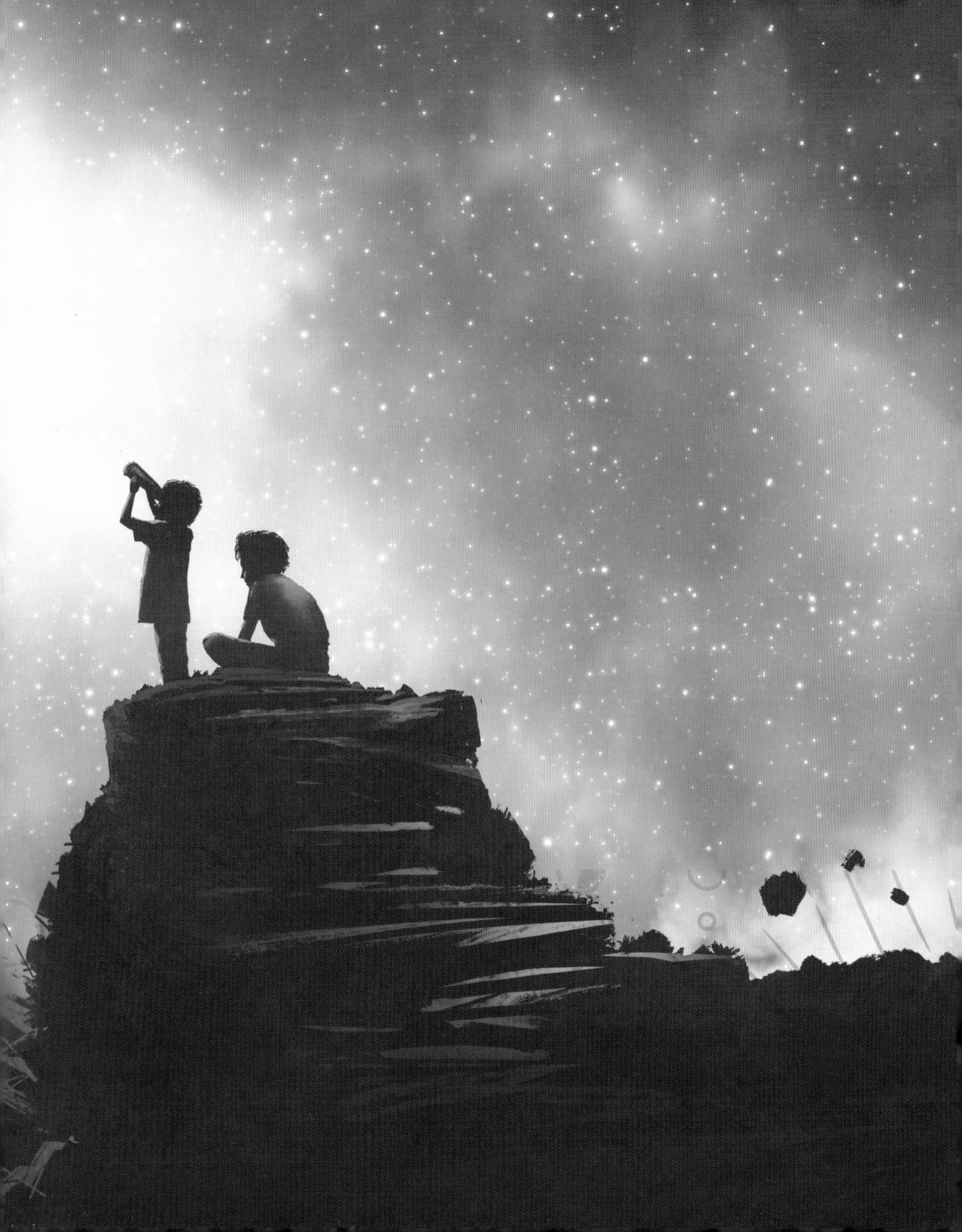

Every choice we make
affects us one way or another.
As people, we either become
overlapped or live simultaneously
apart. However, this is what should
animate us— if we are lucky, the
choices we make can determine
the life that we want to live.